**Editorial Project Manager**
Mara Ellen Guckian

**Editor-in-Chief**
Sharon Coan, M.S. Ed.

**Illustrators**
Alexandra Artigas
Bonnie Bright

**Cover Artist**
Brenda DiAntonis

**Art Manager**
Kevin Barnes

**Art Director**
CJae Froshay

**Imaging**
Ralph Olmedo, Jr.
Rosa C. See
James E. Grace

**Product Manager**
Phil Garcia

**Publisher**
Mary D. Smith, M.S. Ed.

# Patterning & Sequencing

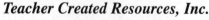

**A B A B**

**Author**

*Jennifer Kern, M.A.*

***Teacher Created Resources, Inc.***
6421 Industry Way
Westminster, CA 92683
www.teachercreated.com.
**ISBN: 978-0-7439-3231-8**
*©2003 Teacher Created Resources, Inc.*
Reprinted, 2012
Made in U.S.A.

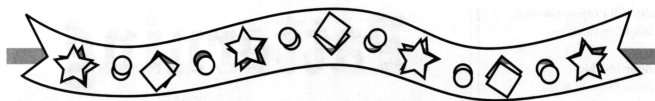

# Table of Contents

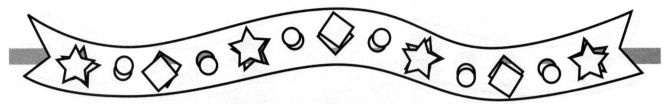

# Introduction

Getting children ready for academic success starts early. It is important, in these early years, to shape children's attitudes towards school and learning in a positive manner. The ultimate purpose of this series is to promote children's development and learning in an exciting manner. Young children need lots of repetition and directions that are worded in a simple format. The activities need to be enjoyable and visually stimulating. This series was developed with those goals in mind. Each activity book is designed to introduce young learners to new concepts and to reinforce ones already learned. The pages are great for enrichment, classroom practice, tutoring, home schooling, or just for fun.

Patterns are part of our everyday lives. Wherever we look, we see patterns. There are patterns in nature, in fabrics, in floor tiles, and even tire tracks! There are patterns in numbers, words, colors, and rhythms. Breaking down patterns and creating or identifying patterns help children begin to break down codes in reading, math, writing, and spelling. Research shows that the brain remembers information more easily when patterns are linked to it. Rhythms and words are easier to remember when they follow a pattern. This is why stories with repetitive patterns of words are so successful in helping children learn to read.

Patterning is not only important, but it is fun. Children can experience patterns by touching objects, by listening to the sounds around them, and by looking at things. Children create patterns themselves throughout the day—during art, when building, and when helping to set the table. There are patterning opportunities everywhere. *Patterning & Sequencing* is an introduction to different types of patterns designed to enhance an awareness of shapes, pictures, letters, numbers, and words.

Repetitive patterns are labeled with letters that designate how many times each symbol is repeated. For instance, the pattern *circle, square, circle, square,* would be labeled as an A B A B pattern. Each circle would be labeled with an "A" and each square would be labeled with "B." A pattern such as *circle, square, square, circle, square, square* would be labeled A B B A B B and so on. Each page is designed to offer practice in the identification and understanding of patterns.

Sequencing is another important standard for young children to understand. Figuring out sequences is vital for solving problems in everyday situations. Children learn to follow directions in a sequence. When giving directions, younger children may be able to follow only a one- to two-step sequence, while other primary students may be able to follow a sequence involving three or four steps. Organization of thoughts is also connected to sequencing. Sequencing the events in a story (beginning, middle, end), retracing steps to find a lost toy, or simply telling someone about a story or an event involves sequencing skills. Time lines are an important form of sequencing often used in social studies. In science, young children can sequence life cycles and steps used in experiments. A variety of activities have been included to help your child use sequencing skills effectively and to give him or her the tools needed to transfer these skills to everyday situations.

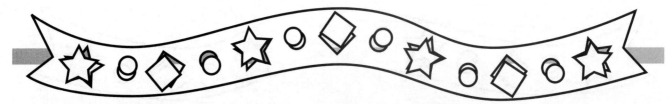

# Identifying AB, ABB, ABC Patterns

As students are exposed to different types of patterns, it is important that they are aware of the number of repetitions that they encounter, and that they are able to make connections between similarities and differences in patterns. To do this, a letter system is used. A pattern that repeats after every two subjects such as *circle, square, circle, square, circle, square* would be identified as an AB pattern. Each circle would be labeled with the letter "A" and each square would be labeled with the letter "B". Students would transfer this each time they encounter two subjects that repeat sequentially. Therefore, when students encounter a pattern of *heart, diamond, heart, diamond, heart, diamond*, it too would be identified as an AB pattern.

Another type of pattern that commonly occurs is an ABB pattern. This is a pattern that uses two subjects, but the second subject is doubled each time. For instance, the AB pattern of *circle, square, circle, square* could become an ABB pattern by doubling the square each time. The ABB pattern is *circle, square, square, circle, square, square*. Again, students can transfer this pattern identification to other areas in which they encounter patterns, allowing them to identify other ABB patterns.

An ABC pattern occurs when three different subjects are repeated in sequential orders. An example of this might include *circle, square, heart, circle, square, heart*. Each *circle* would be labeled with an "A," the *square* with a "B," and a *heart* with a "C."

Of course, letters can be used to identify many different types of patterns and can become as advanced as you wish them to be. The days of the week could be labeled as an ABCDEFG pattern! For this book, we have chosen the AB, ABB, and ABC patterns, which meet educational standards for primary level children.

When practicing the identification of patterns outside of this book, use manipulatives such as coins, silverware, marbles, or crayons. This will help children to transfer what they have learned to real-life situations. Eventually, patterns will help your child to understand his/her world as he or she apply it to time (my birthday comes every 12 months), problem solving (I go to school five days and I have two days off), and math (counting by fives, tens, etc.). These are just a few examples of the benefits of working with patterns. Using letters to identify patterns empowers students to make connections between the different types of patterns they see, helping them to better understand their world.

Name _____

# Square Pattern

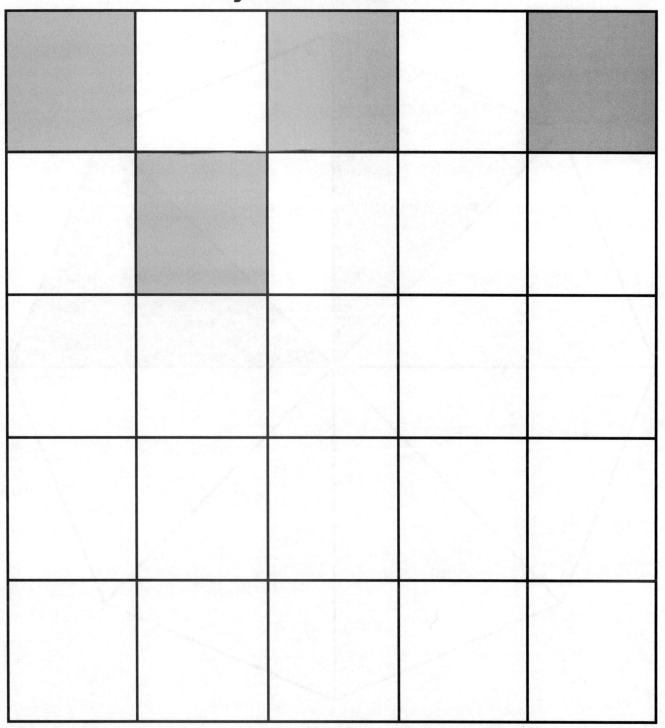

**Directions:** Look at the boxes. A pattern has been started. Choose a color and finish the pattern by coloring the appropriate squares. Color over the gray boxes if you wish.

Name _____

# Triangle Pattern

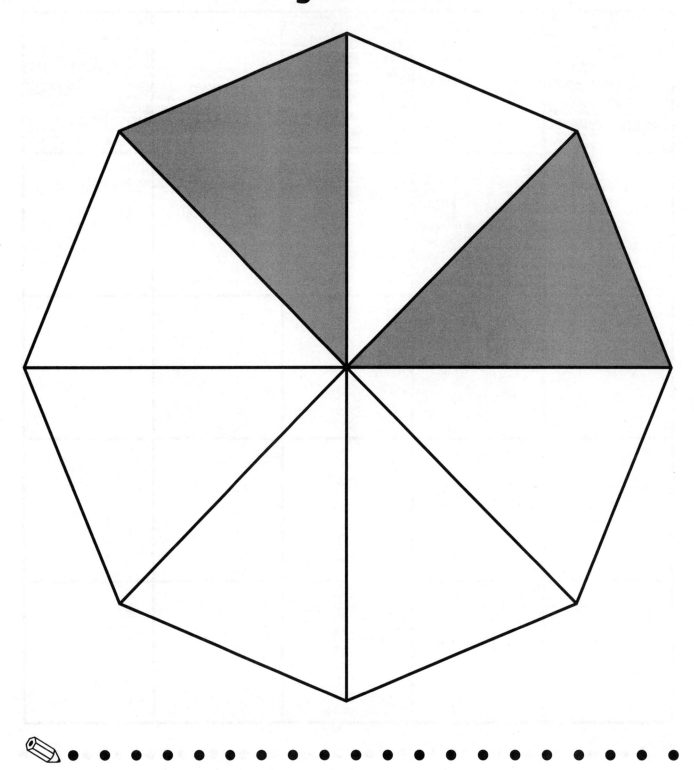

**Directions:** Look at the triangles above. A pattern has been started. Finish the pattern by coloring the appropriate triangles. Color over the gray boxes if you wish.

Name _____

# Flag Pattern

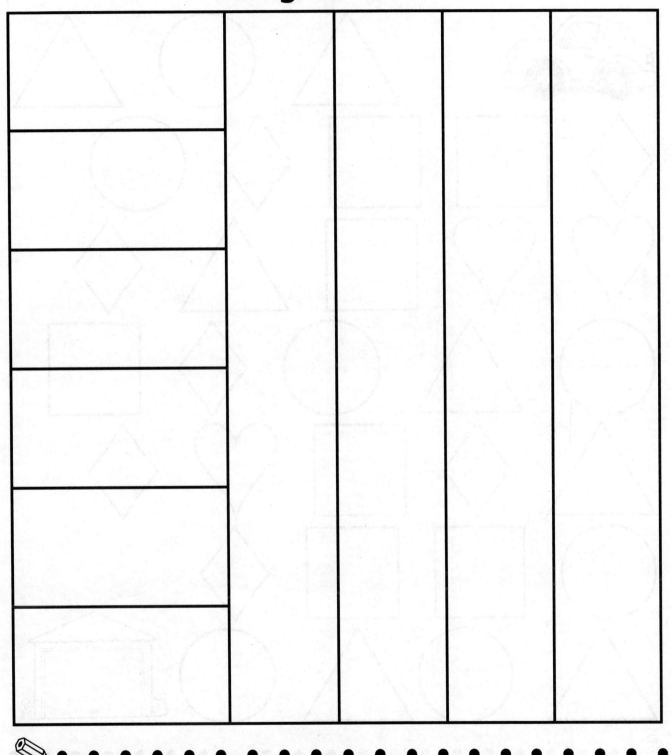

**Directions:** Use two colors to create a pattern on the flag.

# Name _____

# Get on the Road!

**Directions:** Help the car get to the garage by following the △○ pattern through the maze of shapes. Color the AB pattern by using two colors of your choice.

Name _____

# Super Star

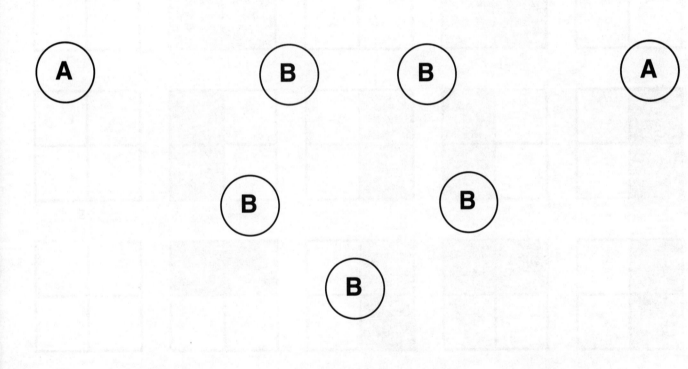

**Directions:** Follow the dots in an AB pattern to create a star. Begin at the top Ⓐ.

Name _____

# Patterning with Squares

**Directions:** Look at each row of squares. Complete the pattern by coloring the last group of squares in each row in the appropriate boxes.

Name _____

# The Pattern Path

**Directions:** Help Little Red find her way through the woods by following the path with a pattern.

Name _____

# Buggy Patterns

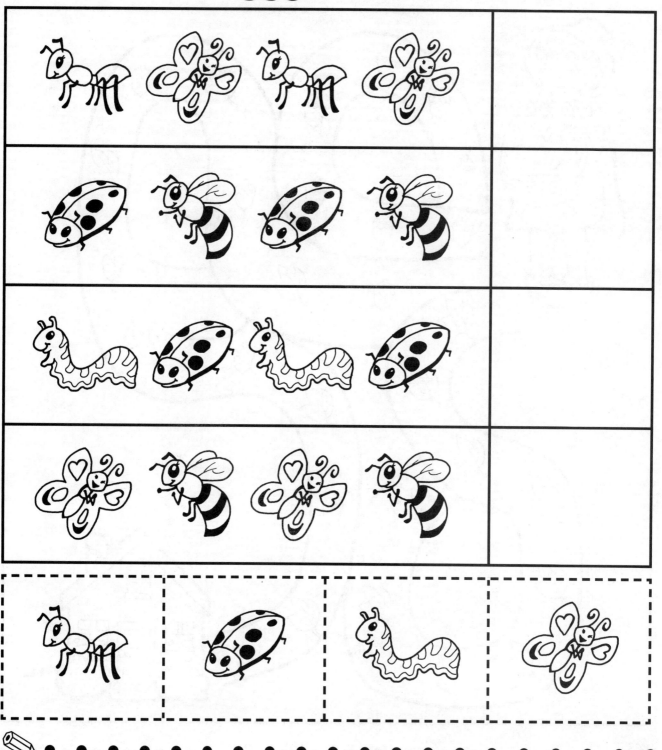

**Directions:** Look at each pattern. Cut out the bugs in the dashed lines. Glue the bug that comes next in each pattern in the space provided.

# Name _____

# Work Out with Patterns!

**Directions:** Look at each AB pattern. Cut out the picture at the bottom of the page that completes each pattern. Glue the picture in the space provided.

Name _____

# Flower Patterns

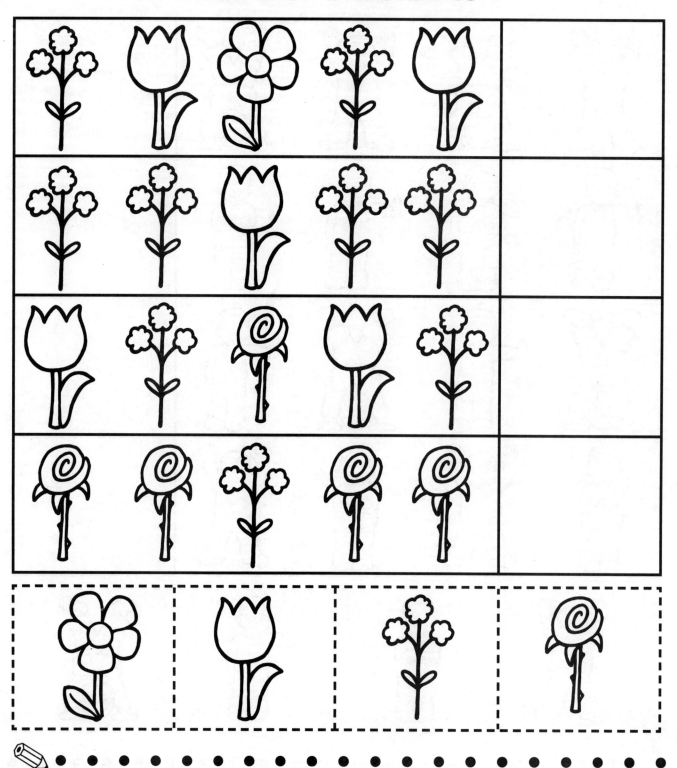

**Directions:** Look at each row of flowers. Determine the pattern in each row. Cut out the flower that comes next in each pattern. Glue the flower in the space provided.

Name _____

# Glasses Patterns

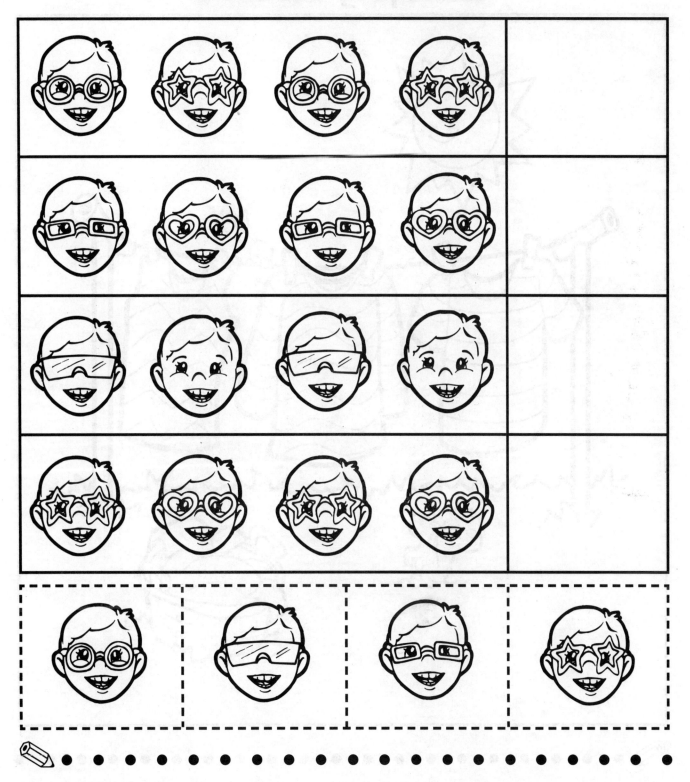

**Directions:** Look at each face. Determine which glasses should go on the last face to complete the pattern. Cut out the face and glasses that come next in each pattern. Glue the face in the space provided.

15

Name _____

# Stripey Shirts

**Directions:** Create a pattern on each shirt using two colors.

# Name _____

# Flag Patterns

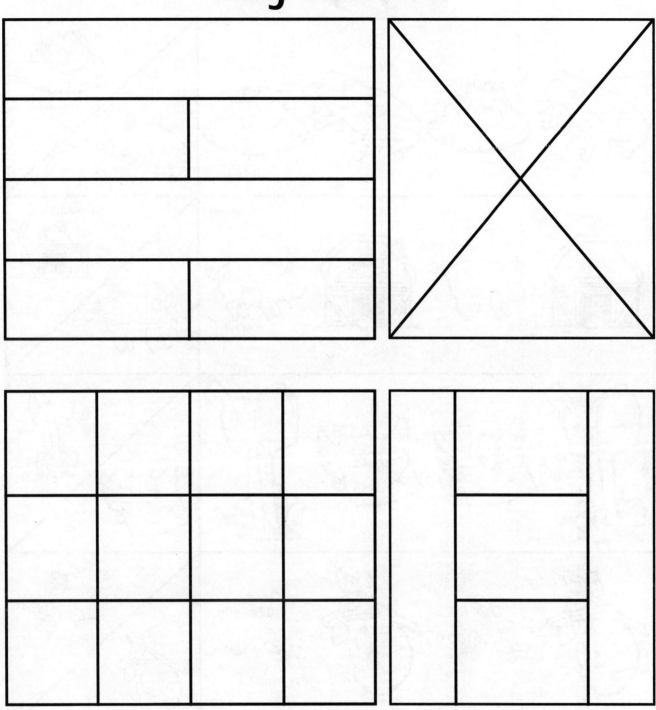

**Directions:** Flags often have patterns of color. Color each flag, creating a pattern on each one.

Name _____

# Plenty of Patterns

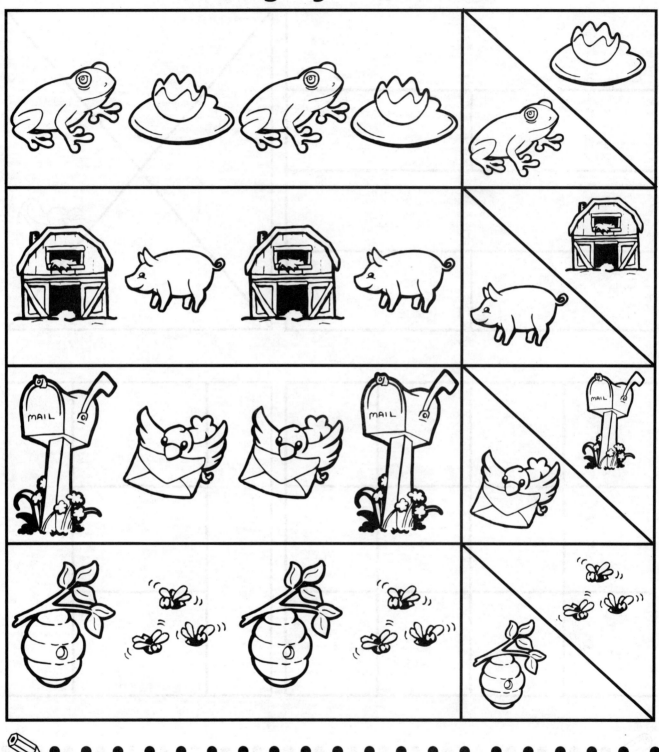

**Directions:** Look at each pattern. Choose the picture in the box with diagonal line that comes next in the pattern. Circle that picture. Color the sequence if time allows.

Name _____

# What Comes Next?

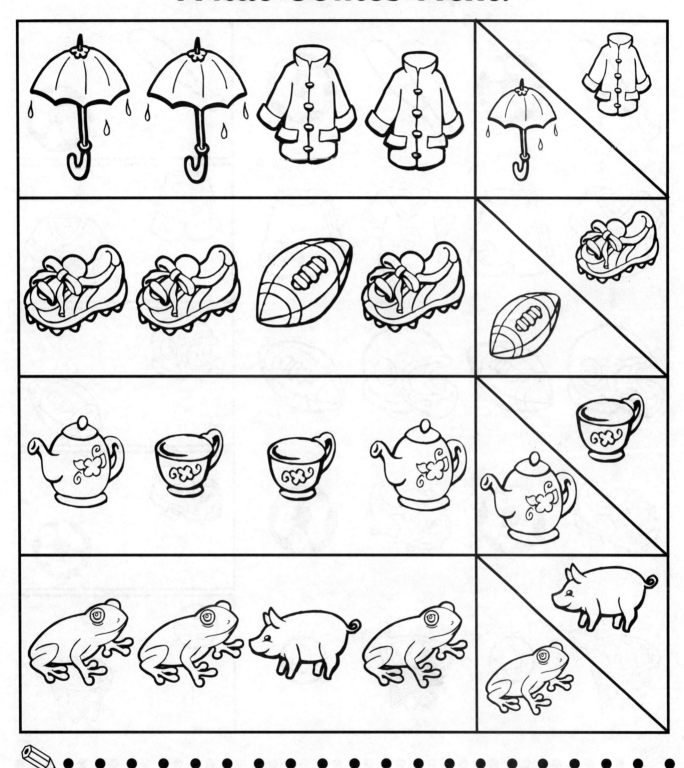

**Directions:** Look at each pattern. Choose the pattern that comes next from the box with the diagonal line. Color the picture that comes next.

Name _____

# Sports Patterns

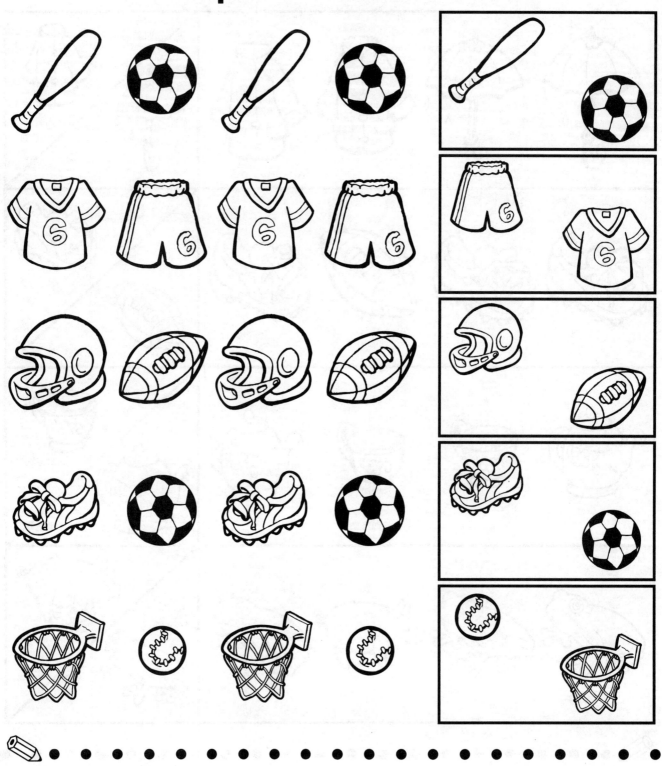

**Directions:** Color each pattern. Complete each pattern by coloring the picture that comes next in the pattern.

Name _____

# Tricky Patterns

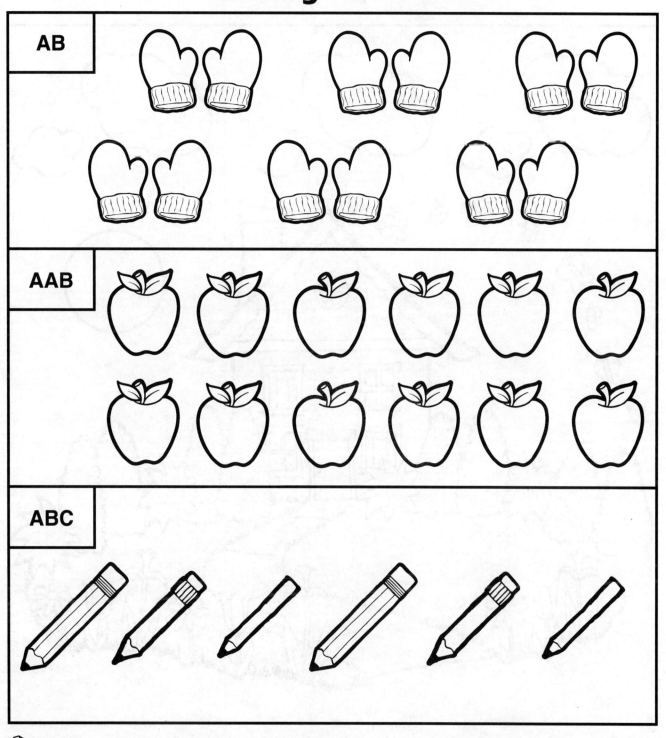

AB

AAB

ABC

**Directions:** Using different color crayons, color the rows of pictures in each box to create the pattern indicated.

Name _____

# Finding Patterns

**Directions:** Find patterns in the picture.  Color the patterns.

Name _____

# Patterns Left and Right

L=Left                    R=Right

**Directions:** Find the patterns of left and right.  Identify each by writing "L" for left and "R" for right.

Name _____

# Number Patterns

1 2 3 1 2 ___

6 9 6 9 ___ 9

5 7 7 5 7 ___

3 4 ___ 3 4 5

9 ___ 9 8 9 8

······································

**Directions:** Look at each line of number patterns. Write the missing number on each line to complete the pattern.

Name _____

# More Number Patterns

2 2 3 3 2

5 6 7 5 6

1 0 0 1 0

8 8 9 9 8

4 2 5 4 2

**Directions:** Look at the patterns of numbers in each line. Complete each pattern by writing the number that comes next in the box provided.

Name _____

# Pick the Pattern

**AB   ABB   ABC**

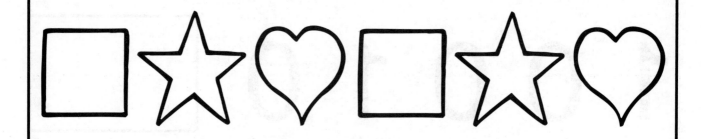

**AB   ABB   ABC**

**AB   ABB   ABC**

**Directions:** Look at each pattern. Decide if the pattern is an AB pattern, an ABB pattern, or an ABC pattern. Circle the correct answer in each row.

Name _____

# Funny Fish

**Key: AB, AABB, ABB, ABC**

**Directions:** Look at the stripe pattern on each fish. Decide if the pattern is AB, AABB, ABB, or ABC. Write the answer in the box.

27

Name _____

# Sneaky Snake

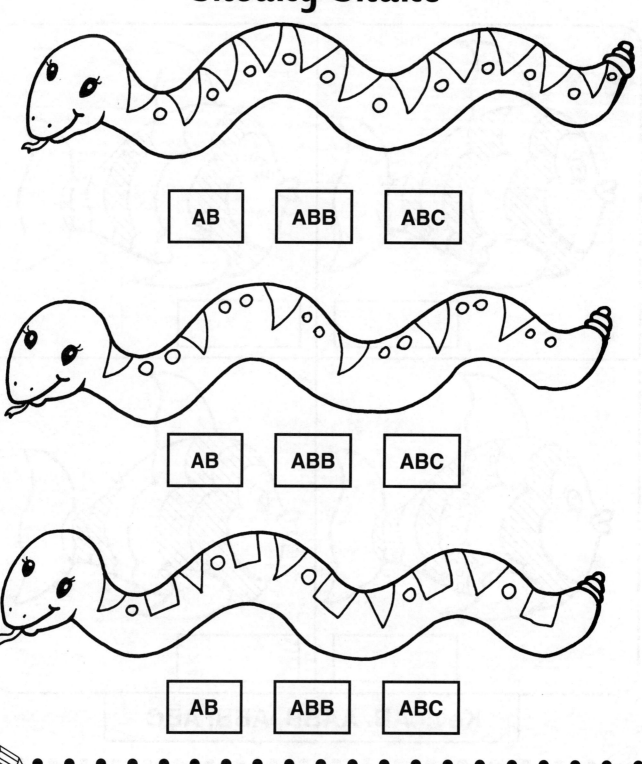

AB    ABB    ABC

AB    ABB    ABC

AB    ABB    ABC

**Directions:** Color the pattern on each snake. Decide if the pattern is an AB pattern, an ABB pattern, or an ABC pattern. Circle the correct answer.

# Color Word Patterns

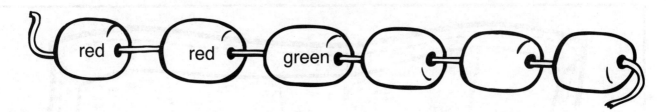

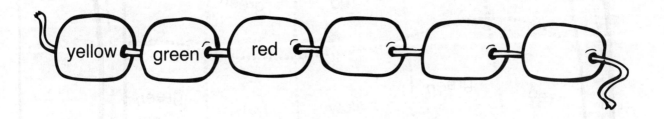

**Directions:** Read each color word. Color the necklaces following the color pattern.

# Name _____

# Quilting

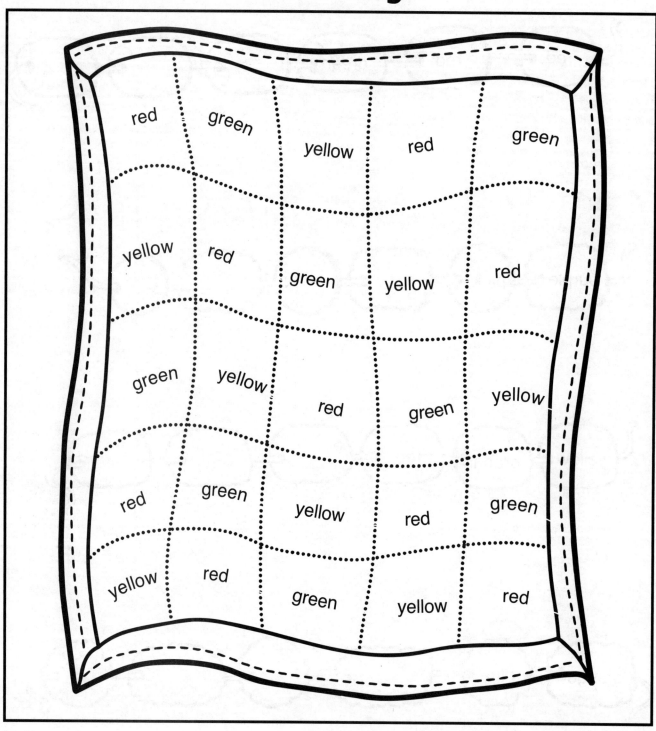

Inside the quilt (top to bottom, left to right):

red  green  yellow  red  green

yellow  red  green  yellow  red

green  yellow  red  green  yellow

red  green  yellow  red  green

yellow  red  green  yellow  red

**Directions:** Look at the color words. Color the pattern to complete the quilt.

Name _____

# Make Your Own Patterns

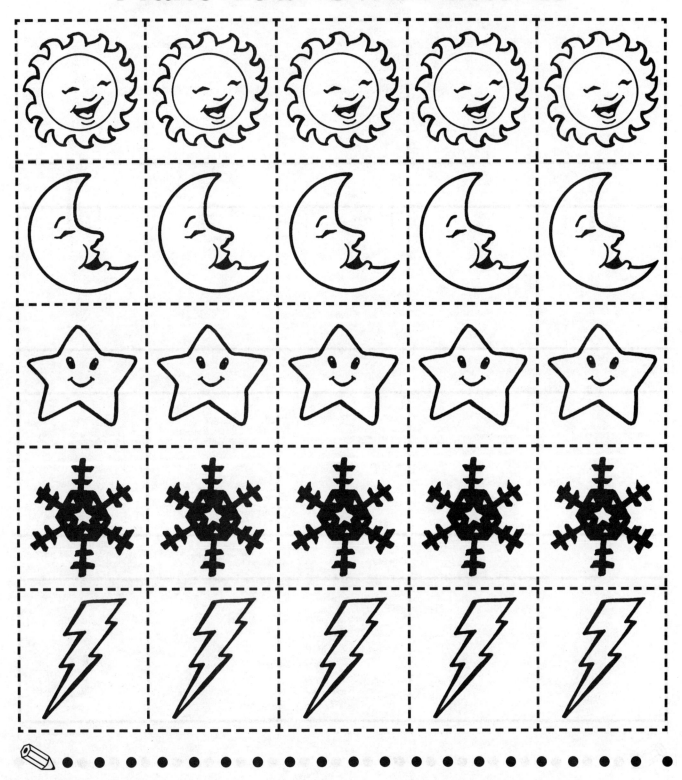

**Directions:** Cut out the pictures above and create your own patterns using the grid on page 32 or on a piece of colored construction paper.

Name _____

# Patterns Grid

**Directions:** Use the grid above with the pattern pieces on page 31. Create your own patterns. You will have pieces left over.

Name _____

# Number Sequence

| 0 | 1 | 2 | ___ |
|---|---|---|---|
| ___ | 8 | 9 | ___ |
| 9 | 10 | ___ | 12 |
| 4 | 5 | ___ | 7 |

| 6 | 3 | 10 | 11 | 7 |
|---|---|---|---|---|

**Directions:** Cut out the dotted-line boxes. Glue the numbers in the spaces provided in the correct sequence for each row.

Name _____

# Letter Sequence

| _ _ | B | _ _ | D | _ _ |
|---|---|---|---|---|
| F | _ | H | I | _ _ |
| K | L | _ _ | N | O |
| _ _ | Q | R | _ _ | T |
| U | _ _ | _ _ | X | Y |

| W | M | J | C | E |
|---|---|---|---|---|
| P | V | S | G | A |

✏️ • • • • • • • • • • • • • • • • • • • • • • • •

**Directions:** Cut out the dotted-line boxes above. Glue the letters in the spaces provided in the correct sequence.

Name _____

# Draw a Bird

| 1 | 2 | 3 |
|---|---|---|
| Draw a large oval. Draw a triangle in the center. | Add eyes and wings. | Draw a feather on the head. Add feet. |

**Directions:** Use the numbered sequence to draw two birds in the frame. Add a background.

Name _____

# Draw a Turtle

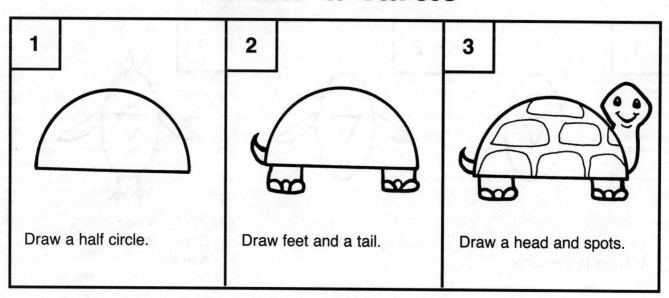

1. Draw a half circle.

2. Draw feet and a tail.

3. Draw a head and spots.

**Directions:** Use the numbered sequence to draw a turtle. Add scenery to your picture.

Name _____

# Growing Up

**Directions:** Cut out the pictures above. Glue them onto a separate strip of paper in order from youngest to oldest.

Name _____

# Seasons

fall

spring

winter

summer

**Directions:** Cut out the pictures of each season. Glue them onto a separate strip of paper in order. Begin with fall. Color the pictures.

38

Name _____

# ABC Order: Food

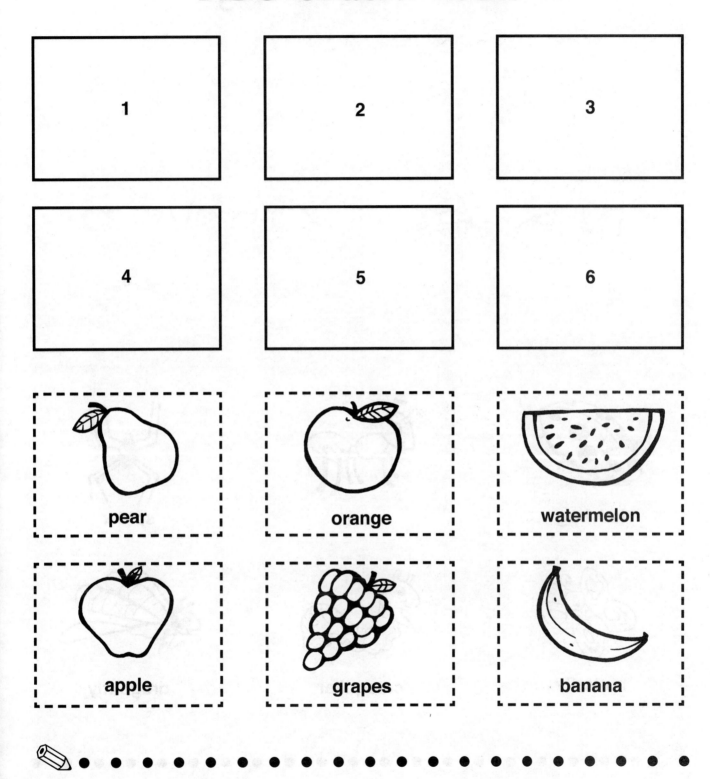

|  |  |  |
|---|---|---|
| 1 | 2 | 3 |
| 4 | 5 | 6 |

pear

orange

watermelon

apple

grapes

banana

**Directions:** Color the fruit. Cut out the pictures. Glue them in the boxes in alphabetical order.

Name _____

# ABC Order:  Bugs

| 1 | 2 | 3 |

| 4 | 5 | 6 |

ladybug

ant

spider

butterfly

caterpillar

dragonfly

**Directions:** Cut out the pictures of the bugs.  Glue them in the boxes in alphabetical order.

Name _____

# Day to Night

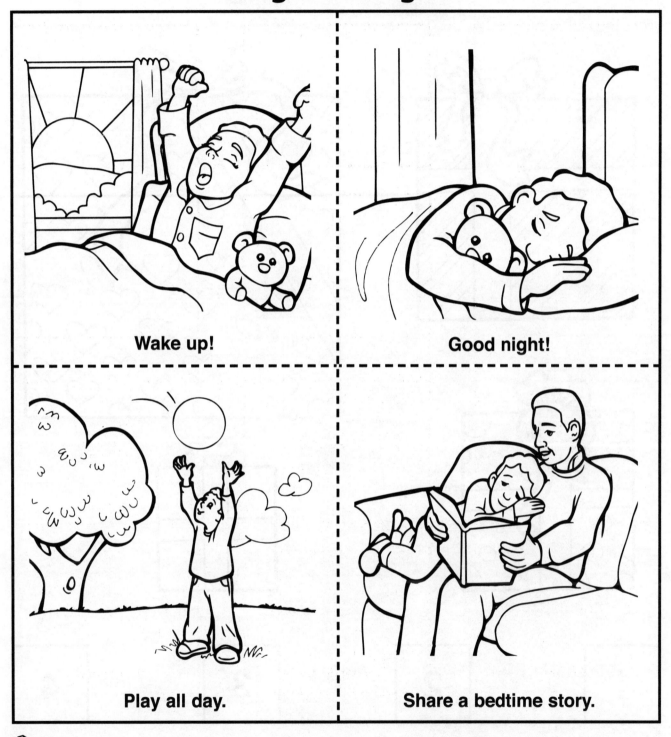

Wake up!

Good night!

Play all day.

Share a bedtime story.

**Directions:** Cut out the pictures. Glue them onto a separate piece of paper in order. Begin with morning.

Name _____

# Small to Big

**Directions:** Put the gifts in order from smallest to biggest by drawing a line from each gift to the number that represents the order. (smallest = 1; largest = 4)

# Time

**Directions:** Draw a line from the clock to the number to show which time comes first, second, third, and fourth. The first one is done for you.

Name _____

# Birthday Cake

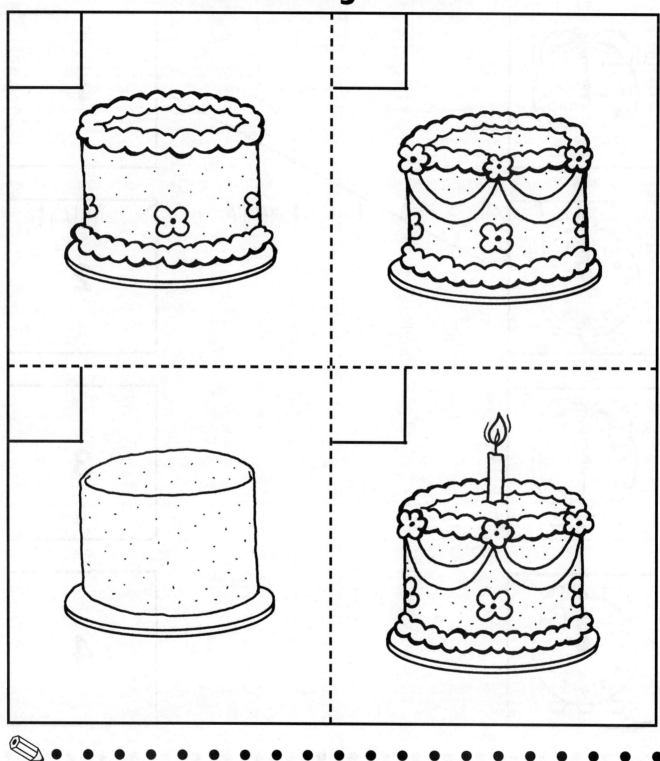

**Directions:** Put the four pictures in order. Write a number in each box.

# Name _____

# Set the Table

**Directions:** Put the four pictures in order. Write a number in each box.

Name _____

# Snowman

**Directions:** Cut out the cards.  Glue the pictures in order on a strip of paper.  Write a number in each box.  Tell the story.

Name _____

# Getting Dressed

**Directions:** Cut out the pictures and arrange them in order. Write numbers in the boxes to show which picture comes first, second, third, fourth, fifth, and sixth. Glue the pictures to a separate piece of paper.

Name _____

# What Comes Next?

**Directions:** Look at the sequence in each row. Look at the two boxes at the end of each row. Circle the picture that comes next in the sequence.